GREAT BOOKS *of the* BIBLE

Philippians

Joy Under Pressure

Tim Stafford

ZondervanPublishingHouse
Grand Rapids, Michigan

A Division of HarperCollins*Publishers*

Philippians: Joy Under Pressure
Copyright © 1995 by Tim Stafford

Requests for information should be addressed to:

ZondervanPublishingHouse
Grand Rapids, Michigan 49530

ISBN: 0-310-49811-2

Cover design by Jeff Sharpton, PAZ Design Group
Interior design by Joe Vriend

Printed in the United States of America

95 96 97 98 99 00 01 02 /❖ DP / 10 9 8 7 6 5 4 3 2 1

CONTENTS

GREAT BOOKS OF THE BIBLE

Every book of the Bible is important, because each one is inspired by God. But certain books draw us to them time and again for their strong encouragement, powerful teaching, and practical wisdom. The Great Books of the Bible Series brings into one collection eight biblical books that distinguish themselves either because of their undisputed excellence or because they are perennial favorites.

The Psalms, with their poetic imagery, help us express our emotions to God and see the myriad ways God works during the best and worst times of our lives. Two books—Proverbs in the Old Testament and James in the New Testament—offer practical wisdom for dealing with the decisions and realities of everyday life. The gospel of John gives us the most intimate and personal view of Jesus, the God-become-man who is Savior and Lord.

Three books are letters written by the apostle Paul. Romans is Paul's masterpiece—the clearest and fullest explanation of the gospel found in Scripture; there we see our world through God's eyes. Philippians shows us how to experience joy when we are under pressure. Ephesians explores the crucial role of the church as a living community, giving us just a little taste of heaven on earth as we seek to serve the Lord.

The series ends where the Bible does—with Revelation, the last book of the Bible, where we glimpse our glorious future, when all things will become new.

Whether you are a new student of God's Word or one who has studied these books many times before, you will find here new insights and fresh perspectives that will make the Bible come alive for you.

The Great Books of the Bible Series is designed to be flexible. You can use the guides in any order. You can use them individually or in a small group or Sunday school class. Some of the guides have six studies; others have as many as thirteen. Moreover, these books help us discover what the Bible says rather than simply telling us the answers. The questions encourage us to think and explore options rather than merely filling in the blanks with one-word answers.

Leader's notes are provided in the back of each guide. They show how to lead a group discussion, provide additional information on questions, and suggest ways to deal with problems that may come up in the discussion. With such helps, someone with little or no experience can lead an effective study.

Suggestions for Individual Study

1. Begin each study with prayer. Ask God to help you understand the passage and to apply it to your life.

2. A good modern translation, such as the *New International Version,* the *New American Standard Bible,* or the *New Revised Standard Version,* will give you the most help. Questions in this guide are based on the *New International Version.*

3. Read and reread the passage(s). You must know what the passage says before you can understand what it means and how it applies to you.

4. Write your answers in the spaces provided in the study guide. This will help you to express clearly your understanding of the passage.

5. Keep a Bible dictionary handy. Use it to look up unfamiliar words, names, or places.

Suggestions for Group Study

1. Come to the study prepared. Careful preparation will greatly enrich your time in group discussion.

2. Be willing to join in the discussion. The leader of the group will not be lecturing, but will encourage people to discuss what they have learned in the passage. Plan to share what God has taught you in your individual study.

3. Stick to the passage being studied. Base your answers on the verses being discussed rather than on outside authorities such as commentaries or your favorite author or speaker.

4. Try to be sensitive to the other members of the group. Listen attentively when they speak, and be affirming whenever you can. This will encourage more hesitant members of the group to participate.

5. Be careful not to dominate the discussion. By all means participate! But allow others to have equal time.

6. If you are the discussion leader, you will find additional suggestions and helpful ideas in the leader's notes at the back of the guide.

JOY UNDER PRESSURE

Not long ago I went walking with a friend of mine, a prominent African lawyer who had been under intense personal pressure in the years since I had last seen him. Fred had taken some political stands that ran contrary to popular opinion. Rumors spread that he had been bribed. He told me that amid the controversy not one Christian friend had come to talk with him—they all had stayed away. His children had felt ostracized at school.

"At first you feel angry and bitter," he told me. "Then you develop a cynical attitude. People may say kind words, but you ask yourself, 'Do they really mean anything?'"

In time, however, Fred gained a very different attitude. "I have had to learn what it means to really love others, regardless of how they act toward me. It's been a very, very valuable lesson. I would not have traded these experiences for anything."

Sometimes hard experiences turn out that way—but not always. Perhaps just as often they lead only to bitterness, anger, and depression. What makes the difference? What enables a person to live under pressure, experiencing crushing disappointment, yet maintaining hope, direction, and joy?

At first glance, Philippians would seem to be the wrong book to answer those questions. Read it over quickly, and you may notice simply joy. It is no wonder so many Christians like the book of Philippians. It is a letter to lift anyone's spirits—just the thing to turn to when you're feeling low and need encouragement. Along with its many inviting memory verses, Philippians is pervaded with passion for the good news about Jesus. The words "joy" and "rejoice" appear repeatedly.

People often miss the book's darker side—signs of trouble that show through cracks in its bright exterior. If you read carefully, you will see that Paul was experiencing extreme pressure when he wrote this book. He had reason to feel dejected and alone rather than joyful.

First, Paul was in a Roman prison. He had apparently been there for some time—long enough for the Philippian Christians to hear about it and send Epaphroditus, one of their members, to help. Paul appears to be waiting for a trial at which he believed humiliation and death were possible outcomes (1:20).

For Paul, so impassioned by his calling, it must have been torture to be pulled out of the work he loved and thrown into jail. He wanted to go everywhere, preach to everyone. Instead, he had to sit, chained to a bored, venal prison guard. Always in the back of Paul's mind was the possibility that his life might end right there—pointlessly and inconclusively, as far as the people around him could see.

Meanwhile, Christians on the outside were taking advantage of Paul's absence. He heard that some preachers had stepped up their work just so they could steal his prominence and gain more followers while he was out of the way. Gloomily Paul wrote, "Everyone looks out for his own interests, not those of Jesus Christ" (2:21). It would be hard to think of a worse assessment from Paul, who had gladly given up everything in the service of Christ.

On top of all that, Paul had received bad news from a church he dearly loved and staked great hopes on—the church at Philippi. Ironically, the news apparently came with Epaphroditus, the man the Philippians had sent to help him. (Epaphroditus had become sick and nearly died, which must have reduced his helpfulness substantially.) Evidently he told Paul the church at Philippi was under great persecution. At the same time, two factions were working hard to lead the church astray. And some of the leading members of the church—two women whom Paul knew and esteemed—were feuding and could not resolve their differences.

It might have seemed to Paul that all his work and all his hopes were in vain.

In such circumstances you would not blame Paul if he wrote a self-pitying letter. You would not be surprised if he wrote an angry letter. Instead he wrote a letter brimming with hope. Why? How?

That is exactly the kind of question to bring to the study of Philippians. How is it possible to have joy under pressure? How can we remain genuinely hopeful when others betray and disappoint us? How

10

can we retain a sense of community and mutual love while living and working with very imperfect people who may even bring hurt?

The answer to these questions, Paul would surely tell us, is Christ. Jesus Christ is the focal point of his letter to the Philippians. In chapter 2, verses 1–11, Paul describes a journey that Jesus took—and that we must, in imitation of him, also take. He describes Jesus' humility—how he became a man and ultimately was put to death. He describes God's raising of Jesus from the dead and exalting him above every creature. Paul believes this journey, first down and then up, is the central fact of history. The "still point of the turning world," God himself, has moved, and so the world that he made and holds together can never be the same.

Living in the light of Christ's life, Paul teaches, Christians cannot help having hope. Even under pressure and assault they have a reference point, a direction, a calling. Because God has called others alongside them, Christians have a community of love.

Through the book of Philippians we catch glimpses of a man and his friends struggling with adversity, yet discovering joy because they are thoroughly "Christ-centered." From studying Philippians we can gain something more than inspiration. We can learn how to live Paul's way—with joy under pressure.

Study 1
Building a Foundation
Philippians 1:1–11

When we added on to our home, the extra construction required strengthening the foundation. We live in California, where preparing for earthquakes is a way of life. New, reinforced concrete had to be poured. Steel rods had to be glued into the old foundation, tying old and new together. All this had to be fastened securely to the house through bolts and clips and metal straps. Now when the earth moves, the whole house will bend and flex as a single, strong unit.

People need strong foundations, too. That is why Paul begins this letter the same way he begins most of his other letters: by emphasizing fundamentals. His very emotional words emphasize his ties to the Christians at Philippi and speak of his frequent prayers. There is love here—love that, Paul prays, will grow increasingly intelligent. This loving fellowship, with Christ and each other, can hold these Christians together no matter how the world is shaking.

1. Think of someone who has had a big part to play in your spiritual growth or, conversely, whom you have greatly influenced. What emotions do you feel for that person, and why?

2. Read Philippians 1:1–11. The apostle Paul had an intense spiritual history with the Christians at Philippi. What words does Paul use to describe his attitudes when he prays for them?

3. What attitudes do *you* typically hold when you pray for people?

   If you don't have Paul's attitudes, how can you become more like him?

4. Paul mentions his "confidence" that the Philippians will carry on in their Christian growth (v. 6). What is the root of this confidence?

5. What does Paul mean in saying that the Philippians "share in God's grace with me" (v. 7)?

   Why does this sense of shared grace undergird their mutual love?

6. Often in our "share and prayer" times we concentrate on illness, jobs, and family problems. What does Paul pray for? How can we embrace this as a better model for our prayers?

7. What does Paul mean when he prays that "love may abound more and more in knowledge and depth of insight" (v. 9)?

   Where and how have you seen this kind of love exhibited?

8. We often build friendships on compatibility. We look for people who are likable to us and whom we admire. On what basis does Paul ground his love for the Philippians—on this, or on something else?

9. Suppose there was someone in the Philippian church whom Paul found especially difficult to get along with. What do you think he would do to gain a joyful and loving attitude toward that person?

10. What would it take for you to develop these kinds of attitudes and feelings for other Christians?

What difference would it make in your life if you *y* develop such attitudes and feelings?

Memory Verse This is my prayer: that your love may abound more and more in knowledge and depth of insight.
—Philippians 1:9

Between Studies

During the next week use Paul's prayer for the Philippians as a model for your own prayers. Think especially of a person with whom you have had an intense spiritual connection. (This could be a parent, a spouse, a relative, a friend, or a pastor.) Ask God each day to give that person a more knowledgeable and insightful love as well as discernment for what is really best in his or her life. Ask God to make that person "pure and blameless" and to fill him or her with "the fruit of righteousness." As you think of this person, try to personalize these requests to the circumstances you know he or she deals with.

STUDY 2
WHEN BAD THINGS HAPPEN

PHILIPPIANS 1:12-30

I n some situations it is common to emphasize the positive and ignore the negative. We see this in family letters at Christmas, in getting reacquainted with old friends at class reunions, and even in our conditioned response when the clerk at the checkout counter greets us routinely with a "How are you today?" We tend to show "good manners" and not burden others with unwanted complaints.

As with much of our correspondence, Paul's letter to the Philippians soon shifts from general greetings to news—bringing his readers up-to-date on what has been happening to him. And surprise, surprise! Paul's news is all positive. It would appear that things are going extremely well.

But how many people reading his letter, then or now, would see it that way? Paul is in prison and potentially facing the death penalty. His "friends" on the outside are acting outrageously. Is Paul's positive thinking just an act—an attempt to look on the bright side no matter what? Is he just being polite? Or does he have a radically different perspective that truly transforms his view of life?

1. Have you ever had what seemed like terrible news turn out to be for the good? What happened to change "bad" into "good"?

2. Read Philippians 1:12–30. The "what has happened" Paul mentions in verses 12 and 19 is his imprisonment. Can you mention several ways in which this situation was "bad" for Paul?

3. Nevertheless, Paul reports that "what has happened" has worked out for good. From Paul's perspective, how did "good" come out of those "bad" things?

4. From Paul's experience, what can we learn about how to make good come out of bad?

5. It seems that Paul's experience reflected in verses 15–18 was not unusual: in times of adversity, people begin criticizing and downgrading others. (See the world of politics for many good examples.) Recall an experience when you have seen that happen. How do you think Paul would advise you to handle the situation?

6. The "good things" we have talked about were related to the building up of a new church—Paul's great mission. But what "good" does Paul seek for himself (vv. 19–20)?

If Paul does not already have the "good things" he longs for, when can he hope to get them?

7. Paul expresses his hope that he will have "sufficient courage." How much courage is that?

How can you tell when you have "sufficient courage"?

8. What does Paul mean, "For me, to live is Christ and to die is gain" (v. 21)? Why can he say this in all sincerity?

9. What "bad" is happening to the Philippians (vv. 29–30)?

10. What good does Paul wish for the Philippians in those bad circumstances?

11. Some religions teach that "bad" is an illusion that can be eliminated by the right kind of thinking. How do you think Paul would respond to that?

12. What can we learn from Paul's example about making good out of a bad situation?

Between Studies

This week look at other Scriptures that demonstrate the transforming perspective of Christ, making good out of bad. Romans 8 is Paul's great hymn to the abundance of benefits Jesus brings in all circumstances. In the Old Testament, Lamentations 3:19–33 is a powerful testimony written from the ashes of Jerusalem after the city had fallen to the Babylonians following a two-year siege. Read these passages and reflect again on the "bad times" you yourself have seen.

STUDY 3
A GOOD ATTITUDE

PHILIPPIANS 2:1-18

When the pressure is on, we can sometimes take action to change the situation. Sometimes, though, we can't do much to change things. Circumstances are out of our control, and we can only wait for God's action to deliver us.

One way to deal with uncontrollable situations is to control our attitudes. Because that can make a tremendous difference, Paul encourages the Philippians to consider the attitude they have toward one another. He offers Jesus as the ultimate example of having the right attitude.

1. When people say, "So-and-so has a good attitude," what do they usually mean by that?

2. Read Philippians 2:1–18. On the basis of these verses, what do you think Paul would describe as his ideal mental attitude?

3. We have seen that the Philippians were under severe pressure, suffering for their faith. In such circumstances we might think a talk on courage would be most needed. Yet Paul's great concern seems to be for humility and church unity—not the first qualities most of us would look for in a crisis. Why do you think Paul considered humility and church unity so important?

4. In verses 1 and 2, what four motives does Paul give for maintaining unity?

5. Paul's four motives are all very experiential—they assume that Christians are being helped by their relationship with Christ. What do you think Paul would say to someone who doesn't feel encouragement, comfort, fellowship, and tenderness?

6. What separates the humility described in verses 3 and 4 from the experience of being a "doormat" or "codependent" or "letting people take advantage of you"?

7. To "consider others better than yourselves" could imply allowing that the other guy is always right and should always have his way. If this is not what verse 3 means, then how is the other person "better"?

8. How would Paul say (v. 4) we should balance our interests with those of other people?

9. Paul holds up Jesus as the ideal example of humility. What events in Jesus' life does he point to? What other events in Jesus' life can you recall from the New Testament that show his great humility?

10. Paul describes the result of Christ's humility in verses 9–10. The way we commonly think of humility might suggest that Jesus should declare, "I don't deserve all this glory." Yet, he doesn't. How can Jesus receive such glory and remain an example of humility?

11. How do you explain verses 10–11 in light of the reality that Jesus Christ is not only ignored but also vehemently rejected by much of the world today? When will Paul's prediction of universal submission to Christ come true?

12. On the basis of Christ's example in this passage, how would you describe humility now?

Memory Verse Your attitude should be the same as that of Christ Jesus: Who, being in very nature God, did not consider equality with God something to be grasped, but made himself nothing, taking the very nature of a servant.

—Philippians 2:5–7

Between Studies

Read through one of the Gospels—Matthew, Mark, Luke, or John—and consider Jesus' example of humility. Sometimes he did not match a conventional idea of humility, as when he rebuked the Pharisees. At other times his humility was hard for his disciples to accept, as when he made time for little children. Looking at as many examples as you can, think about how you can follow Paul's advice that "your attitude should be the same as that of Christ Jesus."

TRUE PARTNERS

PHILIPPIANS 2:12-30

We can become discouraged at our inability to live up to Jesus' example flawlessly. But Paul does not leave the Philippians with only Jesus as a positive example. Instead, he brings them encouragement by commending two people whom they know very well. Timothy and Epaphroditus are down-to-earth models of what Paul wants the Philippians to learn.

1. Who is the most truly humble person you know? Describe how you see that humility expressed.

2. Read Philippians 2:12–18. Here Paul continues to speak of how the Philippians should respond to adversity. What attitudes does Paul insist on in verses 12–14?

3. "Fear and trembling" isn't a very attractive state of mind to most people (v. 12). What does Paul mean?

   Why is "fear and trembling" important?

4. Some would say that we should simply obey, without worrying about how it feels. But Paul is concerned for the proper attitudes. What difference does it make whether we have a grudging or a willing attitude when we obey?

   What does obedience look like when it is done with a complaining spirit? How does it look when done willingly?

5. Verses 12–13 express a renowned paradox of the Christian life: we work at it while God works inside us. How does God's work fit together with *our* work?

6. Notice that God works inside Christians in two ways: "to will and to act" in the way that we should. Why are both necessary?

7. According to Paul, when do Christians "shine like stars" in the universe (v. 15)? How do you see this happening in your church or community?

8. In verse 17 Paul seems to view his portending death as a sacrifice made for the sake of his ministry among the Philippians. How can Paul claim to be "glad and rejoice" under such conditions?

9. Read 2:19–30. How does each of the three persons referred to in this passage—Paul, Timothy, and Epaphroditus— show the humility described in 2:1–11 (see study 3)?

10. What does verse 21 suggest about the problems Paul is confronting?

11. Godly living isn't just a matter of proper attitudes, although it must begin with that. It also requires action. What actions are these three men and the Philippians taking to show their faith?

12. What actions can we take to "work out our salvation" through humility, as these men did?

Memory Verse Do everything without complaining or arguing, so that you may become blameless and pure, children of God without fault in a crooked and depraved generation, in which you shine like stars in the universe as you hold out the word of life.

—Philippians 2:14–16

Between Studies

On a sheet of paper begin making a list of the people whom you see actively "working out their salvation." On the left side, under each person's name describe briefly what you see him or her doing. On the right side, describe the attitude with which he or she does it. See how many names and how many different modes of action you can come up with. What do they have in common? How can you learn from them?

Study 5
Passionate Living

Philippians 3:1 – 4:1

Christians sometimes speak as though their depth of feeling is all that matters in relating to God. They refer back to some time when they loved to read the Bible and pray, when worship could carry them away, when they were "on fire" for the Lord. They look for a way to stir up that passion again.

Passion matters, and Paul is a prime example of a man passionately in love with Christ. This passage shows Paul at his most emotional. At the same time, these verses show that other people were passionately going in the wrong direction. Paul warns strongly against the wrong kind of passion, while giving himself as an example of how to push hard in the right direction.

1. What are you passionate about? The Super Bowl? A clean kitchen floor? Artichokes? Identify what inspires your passion, and why.

2. Read Philippians 3:1–4:1. In this passage Paul shows his passion for Christ. But why does he begin with a passionate warning about some dangerous people (v. 2)?

3. It has been said, "It doesn't really matter what you believe, as long as you're sincere." Why would Paul disagree with that statement?

4. In verse 2 Paul is probably referring to "Judaizers," a faction in the early church who believed that a real Christian had to be an observant Jew, going through circumcision and living by the Old Testament law. Why would this bother Paul so much? What was at stake?

5. In verses 4–6 Paul gives his own life example. What was he passionate about before his conversion?

    Why does he consider those things "rubbish" now (v. 8)?

6. When do our other passions interfere with the passion for Christ?

7. What does Paul want to accomplish with his life, according to verses 10–11?

8. What does Paul mean, "becoming like him [Christ] in his death"? Is Paul seeking martyrdom?

9. In verses 12–14 Paul uses the image of a race to describe his life. Where in the race is he? What is the finish line? What is the prize?

10. What do you think Paul is trying to tell the Philippians through this racetrack image?

11. In verses 18–19 Paul warns against another group of people, apparently different from the Judaizers. What is their passion?

12. Do you see the opposition of verses 18–19 at work today? Where and how is it expressed?

13. In contrast, what passionately moves the "citizens of heaven" (v. 20)?

14. Paul was clearly an activist, but he ends this passage by talking about a passionate waiting. What is Paul waiting for? How does this fit with the "pressing on toward the goal" he mentioned earlier?

Memory Verse One thing I do: Forgetting what is behind and straining toward what is ahead, I press on toward the goal to win the prize for which God has called me heavenward in Christ Jesus.

—Philippians 3:13–14

Between Studies

This week consider Jesus as an example of a passionate person. Read through one of the Gospels—Matthew, Mark, Luke, or John—to see what he was passionate about in his own life direction and in what he called others to care about. Ask yourself: Am I passionate about what Jesus was passionate about? How can a passion for the right things help someone live joyfully under pressure?

LESSON
6
THE BOTTOM LINE

PHILIPPIANS 4:2-23

Throughout this letter to the Philippians, Paul expresses geat concern about a number of things. There are joy and warmth and excitement in his tone, but there is also a sense of urgency. Keep in mind that Paul thought he might be executed before the Philippians even received the letter. This was the last chance he would have to help them through their troubles.

Read each word in this last chapter the way Paul must have meant it—as a final, crucial, parting thought.

1. When you were growing up, what was your parents' "bottom line"—the quality or behavior they were determined you should show, no matter what?

2. Read Philippians 4:2–23. How would you summarize Paul's bottom line—the quality or behavior he is determined the Philippians should show, no matter what?

3. How does Paul seem to feel about Euodia and Syntyche as he deals with the quarrel between these women? How does Paul advise that their quarrel should be resolved?

4. Paul has already recommended "rejoicing in the Lord" (3:1). Why does he come back to this in verse 4 in such emphatic terms? What is so important about rejoicing?

5. For you, what interferes with rejoicing? What helps you to rejoice?

6. In verse 6 Paul recommends prayer instead of worrying. What is the result he promises?

7. Paul's plea to "guard your hearts and minds" suggests that there is an evil attacking the Philippians. How would you describe that evil? What is the result when God's peace (*shalom*) *doesn't* guard your mind and heart?

8. In verse 8 Paul recommends that we maintain a positive focus to our thoughts. How does this differ from "the power of positive thinking"?

9. Earlier, in chapter 2, Paul held up Jesus as a model for our attitudes. Why does he now refer his readers to himself as a model (v. 9)?

10. This appeal to look at him could be regarded as egotistical. Why is this not so of Paul? Consider some situations in which it is right—and even necessary—to offer yourself as a model.

11. Read 4:10–19 and refer back to 2:19–30 and 1:12–18 to give a brief history of the relationship between Paul and the church at Philippi.

12. What has pleased Paul so much about the letter and the help he has received?

13. Paul proclaims his own contentment in every circumstance. In a practical sense, what is his secret?

How would you apply this "secret" to your own life?

Memory Verse Do not be anxious about anything, but in everything, by prayer and petition, with thanksgiving, present your requests to God. And the peace of God, which transcends all understanding, will guard your hearts and your minds in Christ Jesus.

—Philippians 4:6–7

Between Studies

It would be a good idea, now that you have completed this study of Philippians, to write down some of the lessons you have learned about living with joy under pressure. Try to express in one sentence the central message this book has for you. Then make a list of the points in Paul's advice that you would like to remember the next time you are under pressure. Keep the list in a place where you will remember it—perhaps in your Bible—so that you can refer to it later.

LEADER'S NOTES

Leading a Bible discussion—especially for the first time—can make you feel both nervous and excited. If you are nervous, realize that you are in good company. Many biblical leaders, such as Moses, Joshua, and the apostle Paul, felt nervous and inadequate to lead others (see, for example, 1 Cor. 2:3). Yet God's grace was sufficient for them, just as it will be for you.

Some excitement is also natural. Your leadership is a gift to the others in the group. Keep in mind, however, that other group members also share responsibility for the group. Your role is simply to stimulate discussion by asking questions and encouraging people to respond. The suggestions listed below can help you to be an effective leader.

Preparing to Lead

1. Ask God to help you understand and apply the passage to your own life. Unless that happens, you will not be prepared to lead others.

2. Carefully work through each question in the study guide. Meditate and reflect on the passage as you formulate your answers.

3. Familiarize yourself with the leader's notes for the study. These will help you understand the purpose of the study and will provide valuable information about the questions in the study.

4. Pray for the various members of the group. Ask God to use these studies to make you better disciples of Jesus Christ.

5. Before the first meeting, make sure each person has a study guide. Encourage them to prepare beforehand for each study.

Leading the Study

1. Begin the study on time. If people realize that the study begins on schedule, they will work harder to arrive on time.

2. At the beginning of your first time together, explain that these studies are designed to be discussions, not lectures. Encourage everyone to participate, but realize that some may be hesitant to speak during the first few sessions.

3. Read the introductory paragraph at the beginning of the discussion. This will orient the group to the passage being studied.

4. Read the passage aloud. You may choose to do this yourself, or you might ask for volunteers.

5. The questions in the guide are designed to be used just as they are written. If you wish, you may simply read each one aloud to the group. Or you may prefer to express them in your own words. Unnecessary rewording of the questions, however, is not recommended.

6. Don't be afraid of silence. People in the group may need time to think before responding.

7. Avoid answering your own questions. If necessary, rephrase a question until it is clearly understood. Even an eager group will quickly become passive and silent if they think the leader will do most of the talking.

8. Encourage more than one answer to each question. Ask, "What do the rest of you think?" or "Anyone else?" until several people have had a chance to respond.

9. Try to be affirming whenever possible. Let people know you appreciate their insights into the passage.

10. Never reject an answer. If it is clearly wrong, ask, "Which verse led you to that conclusion?" Or let the group handle the problem by asking them what they think about the question.

11. Avoid going off on tangents. If people wander off course, gently bring them back to the passage being considered.

12. Conclude your time together with conversational prayer. Ask God to help you apply those things that you learned in the study.

13. End on time. This will be easier if you control the pace of the discussion by not spending too much time on some questions or too little on others.

More suggestions and help are found in the book *Leading Bible Discussions* (InterVarsity Press). Reading it would be well worth your time.

Study	*Building a Foundation*
One	Philippians 1:1–11

Purpose To see how deep, Christ-centered relationships and prayer build a strong foundation for Christians under pressure.

Question 1 This "warm-up" question should help your group realize that the warm emotions Paul expresses (and which some might conclude are "phony") are not so far from their own experience. Ordinarily, people we have been spiritually involved with, even if only for a short time, are people for whom we have strong feelings.

Question 2 In discussing Paul's feelings for the Philippians, you might want to refer to Acts 16:11–40, which describes the beginnings of Paul's relationship to them. The conversion of the Philippian jailer and his family would be especially unforgettable to all involved. You might also want to refer forward to Philippians 4:15–16, which briefly mentions how the relationship continued. It is easy to see why Paul had such strong feelings for these people!

Question 3 Often people pray with a heart full of worry and concern—even anxiety. Paul's thankfulness can revolutionize their prayers.

Question 4 Paul's confidence in the Philippians' growth is rooted in his confidence in God. What God starts, he can be counted on to finish. When we study chapter 2 we will see that Christ's death and resurrection are the foundation for this confidence.

Question 5 Although in one sense Paul is the teacher and the Philippians are the students—he the evangelist and they the evangelized—in a wider sense Paul is intensely aware that "there is level ground at the foot of the cross." Paul never forgot that he had been saved through God's incredible mercy expressed on the road to Damascus (Acts 9:1–19). He had something of the same feelings toward other Christians that survivors of a plane crash, for instance, have toward one another.

Question 6 It is not wrong to pray about illness, jobs, and the like. Often, however, these mundane matters receive all our prayer attention while deeper concerns such as those Paul expresses are neglected.

Question 7   Our view of love tends to be sentimental and emotional, so this question may prove difficult. It is worth struggling with, nevertheless. One way to approach it is to ask, "Have you ever seen love that is thoroughly lacking in knowledge and insight?"

Question 10   The key to developing attitudes like Paul's is adopting his "Christ-centered" mindset. He really does care about the gospel more than anything else. The question becomes, then, how we can become more Christ-centered. This question may lead into a discussion of spiritual disciplines.

Study
Two

When Bad Things Happen

Philippians 1:12–30

Purpose   To see how bad experiences have beneficial results when they are seen through the lens of Christian faith.

Question 1   For example, many people can tell about being turned down at schools, jobs, and promotions, only to discover upon looking back that the place they ended up was far better suited to them. The news had been "bad" only because they lacked a full understanding of the situation. With hindsight they could see it as a positive, even if painful, direction.

Question 2   A Roman prison was no motel. Paul almost certainly suffered physical deprivation, and he feared for his life. Probably just as difficult for Paul would be the fact that he could not do his work. Paul was the man most responsible for spreading the good news about Jesus through the Mediterranean region. He had started many churches and felt deeply responsible for them. It must have been agonizing for him to be locked up and unable to accomplish the urgent tasks he had in mind to do.

Finally, his imprisonment had unleashed all kinds of ugly attitudes among fellow Christians. Some were using his absence as an opportunity to raise their own status and to diminish Paul's. This, too, must have been hard for Paul to take.

Question 3   Paul seized the opportunity set before him, telling his guards about Jesus. How else could he have preached to such people? Regarding his Christian rivals, Paul took a wider perspective. Their motives were regrettable, but more significant was the continuing spread of the gospel. Paul tried to discern God's work going on, even through the disappointments of life.

Question 4 Whatever our circumstances, we should make the most of the opportunities (however limited) we have. We should also try to find an overarching good we can be thankful for.

Question 6 Paul hopes for deliverance, by which he does not seem to mean simply release from prison. Paul is concerned that he have enough courage to face his trial, to act as he ought to, and to witness effectively for Christ. He is confident that God will give him these "goods," but he doesn't have them yet.

Question 10 Paul wishes for the Philippians his company (v. 26), unity among themselves (v. 27), and courage (v. 28).

Question 11 Paul is a realist who never pretends that suffering is an illusion. He deals with it, not by ignoring it or pretending it doesn't exist, but by looking at it through the transforming perspective of Christ.

Question 12 We can learn from Paul's example

— To make the most of whatever opportunities are available
— To pray for courage
— To seek fellowship with other Christians (and pursue the unity that fellowship requires)
— To focus on Christ's glory through our conduct rather than focusing on our own welfare
— To focus on our ultimate desire for fellowship with Christ

Study
Three

A Good Attitude

Philippians 2:1–18

Purpose To understand Jesus as the perfect example of the attitude of humility, a key to living well in pressured situations.

Question 4 The motives for Christian unity that Paul mentions are

— Encouragement in being united with Christ
— Comfort from Christ's love
— Fellowship with the Spirit
— Tenderness and compassion

Question 5 Paul would say that people who cannot relate to these four motives are missing out on much that the Christian life has to offer.

Leaders should be aware that this question may bring some painful feelings to the surface if members of a group feel that their life lacks these qualities. But it is better to face these problems than to pretend they are unimportant. For Paul, the Christian life was a matter of joyful experience as well as correct doctrine. Facing up to this may lead Christians to reexamine their faith and pursue a deeper life in God.

Question 6 Codependent people are really self-oriented. They let others take advantage of them because they are afraid to lose relationship or significance. They hang on at all costs, loving to be needed. A truly humble person has a good self- image, such that he or she is not overly concerned with self. Rather, humble people are concerned about others' well-being. Their focus is outward, beyond themselves.

Question 7 To "consider others better than yourselves" means putting their honor and status above your own. You are willing to be a servant to their real needs.

Question 9 Paul particularly points to the incarnation and the crucifixion as exemplifying Jesus' humility. Some other events in the Gospels are Jesus' healing and feeding people even when he was tired; his putting up with his disciples' slowness and selfishness; his healing lepers, who were unclean according to the ceremonial law; his talking at length to the Samaritan woman; his ministering to crowds of ordinary people instead of high-ranking, wealthier, or better-educated people.

True Partners

Philippians 2:12–30

Purpose To explore further the attitudes Christians should have, and to see these at work in some of Paul's companions.

Question 3 The expression "fear and trembling" does not suggest terror, but rather reverence and respect for God, a recognition that he is God and we are not. This attitude is a natural companion to true humility.

Question 4 When people obey God without these attitudes, they do it either grudgingly or legalistically. In the case of grudging obedience they seem to think they are doing God a favor to obey him. In legalistic obedience they seem to forget that they are serving a personal God. Obedience then becomes just dutifully following rules. In either case, people lose the life-giving perspective that transforms pressure situations.

Question 5 Perhaps no one can fully understand the connections between our choices and God's—this is the mystery of his predestination working with our free will. We do know that the two must always work together. God never "makes" us choose what we don't want; conversely, we are constitutionally incapable of choosing what is good for us unless God gives us the desire for it.

Question 6 To want to do what is right without being able to creates terrible personal frustration. To do what is right without the inner desire for it is cold legalism. Neither one is pleasing to God.

Question 7 The answer to this question takes us back to the previous verse: the lack of grumbling or complaining is the key to developing a shining character.

Question 8 Paul is alluding to Old Testament sacrifice, in which a drink offering was sometimes poured over the meat of an animal as it was placed on the altar to be burned. Because Paul believed that all of life should be a sacrifice to God, he saw nothing strange or ultimately "unfair" about giving his life for the cause of the gospel.

Question 11 Besides his continuing evangelism, Paul has been extending love and concern for Epaphroditus and the Philippians.

Timothy has been faithful in taking a genuine interest in other people—even people far out of his sight. Epaphroditus has made a long journey on his church's behalf to "help out" Paul during his imprisonment. All three in their own ways were men whose priorities revolved around other people.

Study Five   *Passionate Living*
Philippians 3:1–4:1

Purpose   To see Paul as a passionate man whose life was transformed by his desire to know Christ, and at the same time to see that passion for the wrong goals can lead people fatally astray.

Question 3   Paul would be the last one to think that it doesn't matter what you believe as long as you're sincere. He had been a very sincere persecutor of Christians before being turned around on the road to Damascus. You may find it helpful to review Paul's early career as an anti-Christian in Acts 8:1–3 and 9:1–9. Paul knew that people could be very sincerely mistaken and, with all the religious conviction in the world, oppose God's work.

Question 4   The Judaizers, by insisting that non-Jews live up to the Old Testament law, were in effect saying that Christ's death for the forgiveness of sins, and the life he gives through his living Holy Spirit, were not enough to please God. As a godly Jew, Paul knew that living according to Old Testament rules could never please God or change a sinner's basic makeup. For a more complete (and equally passionate) explanation of this issue, refer to Paul's letter to the Galatians.

Question 6   Passions interfere with a passion for Christ when they run contrary to Christ (as in Paul's persecution of Christians) and when they preoccupy us so we cannot see Christ.

Question 8   Paul is referring to the utter humility demonstrated by Jesus at his crucifixion, just the way Paul described it in Philippians 2:5–8.

Question 9   Although Paul may suspect he is near the end of his "race," all he can say for sure is that he is in the thick of it. The finish line will be the time when God has done all he wants to do with him on earth and takes him to heaven. The prize is the approval of the Lord Jesus himself and the glory associated with that.

Question 10   Among other things, Paul is telling the Philippians that if they concentrate on the race they are in, they won't have time to fight with each other. He is trying to help them put their eyes on something beyond their present circumstances: on Christ and the future he wants them to have. Paul also wants them to recognize that personal discipline is required for running in races.

Question 11   This second group of people seems to live for pleasure. Paul may have in mind specifically the Epicureans, the renowned hedonists in Greek society.

Question 14   That Paul is waiting for a Savior even while "pressing on toward the goal" is a paradox very like the one expressed in Philippians 2:13. God is ultimately the only hope we have. His action must save us; we cannot save ourselves. Yet he saves us by working in us, and we have work to do in this. We have to press on toward the goal even while looking for Jesus to come to us.

Study Six

The Bottom Line

Philippians 4:2–23

Purpose   To reflect on the primary quality or behavior that Paul most urgently wants his fellow Christians to demonstrate while they are under pressure.

Question 1   For example, parents care most of all that their children work hard, exhibit good manners, get good grades, stay out of trouble.

Question 2   Paul's "bottom line" might be expressed in several different ways. Essentially he is concerned that Christians be Christ-centered rather than self-centered and that this express itself in humility, gentleness, and joy.

Question 3   Paul describes these women as peers—fellow workers in the church. In light of his strong feelings for the Philippian church, which he expressed in both the first chapter and in this one, we can assume that he cared deeply for Euodia and Syntyche.

Paul says the women should "agree in the Lord." That is to say, they should find common ground in their faith as Christians and let that center pull them together. To accomplish this, they will probably need the intervention of other Christians.

Question 4   Rejoicing, like thanksgiving, focuses on the Lord and his goodness. This helps to put anxieties and problems into perspective and to give us a proper attitude.

Question 8   Paul emphasizes "right" and "pure" thoughts, not simply positive ones. More significantly, he doesn't think the thought process has power in itself. Rather, he encourages Christians to think about the things that are ultimately powerful: the good things that God has done, is doing, and will yet do.

Question 9   The Philippians are personally acquainted with Paul, whereas they have only heard about Jesus. All of us need models from whom we can learn through direct human relationships.

Question 10   When teaching someone to swim, we will not say, "I'm the greatest swimmer who ever lived." That would be egotistical. We will say, "Do it the way I'm doing it."

Question 11   Paul brought the gospel to Philippi on his first venture into Europe, starting a church at Lydia's house but being forced to move on after the conversion of the Philippian jailer (Acts 16). After that, the Philippians were unusually interested in Paul's ministry, supporting him with gifts on multiple occasions. Apparently this relationship had lapsed until they heard that Paul was in prison and sent Epaphroditus carrying gifts to help him. Now Paul was sending Epaphroditus back to them (possibly carrying this letter) and was planning to send Timothy, his trouble-shooting right-hand man, very soon.